March 2016
MW01626075
The Happiness you feel right now can last forever as you apply the Atonement every day!
Happy Easter!
Love you so much!!
Mom

#Feel the Love of your Savior
#He Heals us!

Cover and interior designed by Christina Marcano.

All photography courtesy of istockpotography.com

Published by Covenant Communications, Inc.
American Fork, Utah

Printed in China
First Printing: March 2016
22 21 20 19 18 17 16 10 9 8 7 6 5 4 3 2 1

ISBN-13: 978-1-68047-940-9

THE *Atonement*

Messages of Hope, Healing, and Happiness

The Savior has suffered not just for our iniquities but also for the inequality, the unfairness, the pain, the anguish, and the emotional distresses that so frequently beset us. There is no physical pain, no anguish of soul, no suffering of spirit, no infirmity or weakness that you or I ever experience during our mortal journey that the Savior did not experience first. You and I in a moment of weakness may cry out, "No one understands. No one knows." No human being, perhaps, knows. But the Son of God perfectly knows and understands, for He felt and bore our burdens before we ever did. And because He paid the ultimate price and bore that burden, He has perfect empathy and can extend to us His arm of mercy in so many phases of our life. He can reach out, touch, succor—literally run to us—and strengthen us to be more than we could ever be and help us to do that which we could never do through relying upon only our own power.

—David A. Bednar

And we talk of Christ, we rejoice in Christ, we preach of Christ, we prophesy of Christ, and we write according to our prophecies, that our children may know to what source they may look for a remission of their sins.

—2 Nephi 25:26

When we are racked
or harrowed up or
tormented by guilt or
burdened with grief,
He can heal us.
While we do not fully
understand how the
Atonement of Christ
was made, we can
experience the peace of
God which passeth all
understanding.

—BOYD K. PACKER

Come, Saints, and
drop a tear or two
For him who groaned
beneath your load;
He shed a thousand
drops for you,
A thousand drops of
precious blood.

—"He Died! The Great Redeemer Died"

Having "descended below all things," He comprehends, perfectly and personally, the full range of human suffering! A spiritual sung in yesteryear has an especially moving and insightful line: "Nobody knows the troubles I've seen, nobody knows but Jesus." Truly, Jesus was exquisitely "acquainted with grief," as no one else.

—Neal A. Maxwell

Every saint has a past, and every sinner has a future.

—OSCAR WILDE

Oh sweet the joy this sentence gives, I know that my Redeemer lives. May the whole world know it and live by that knowledge I humbly pray.

—THOMAS S. MONSON

The Savior's Atonement will overcome and compensate for all of the unfairness of mortal life.

—QUENTIN L. COOK

And again, if ye by the grace of God are perfect in Christ, and deny not his power, then are ye sanctified in Christ by the grace of God, through the shedding of the blood of Christ, which is in the covenant of the Father unto the remission of your sins, that ye become holy, without spot.

—Moroni 10:33

In a day when the winds are blowing and the waves beating upon our ship, how do we navigate our course safely into the peaceful harbor? What must we do to have our Savior pilot us through tempestuous seas? Amidst the babble of voices—enticing voices which threaten to lead us into forbidden paths or which beckon us to labor in secondary causes, how do the Saints of the Most High know the Way, live the Truth, and gain that Life which is abundant?

. . . We must learn to trust in him more, in the arm of flesh less. We must learn to rely on him more, and on man-made solutions less. We must learn to surrender our burdens to him more. We must learn and work to our limits and then be willing to seek that grace or enabling power which will make up the difference, that sacred power which indeed makes all the difference!

—Robert L. Millet

So Christ was once offered to bear the sins of many; and unto them that look for him shall he appear the second time without sin unto salvation.

—Hebrews 9:28

We all depend on the Savior; none of us can be saved without Him. Christ's Atonement is infinite and eternal. Forgiveness for our sins comes with conditions. We must repent, and we must be willing to forgive others. . . . Remember, heaven is filled with those who have this in common: They are forgiven.

And they forgive. Lay your burden at the Savior's feet. Let go of judgment. Allow Christ's Atonement to change and heal your heart. Love one another. Forgive one another.

The merciful will obtain mercy.

—Dieter F. Uchtdorf

Moreover, Jesus not only took upon Him our sins to atone for them, but also our sicknesses and aching griefs. Hence, He knows personally all that we pass through and how to extend His perfect mercy—as well as how to succor us. His agony was all the more astonishing in that He trod "the wine-press alone."

—Neal A. Maxwell

The atoning sacrifice of the Savior is what makes perfection or sanctification possible. We could never do it on our own, but God's grace is sufficient to help us.

—Larry R. Lawrence

Behold, I have graven thee upon the palms of my hands; thy walls are continually before me.

—1 Nephi 21:16

He is Jesus Christ the holy one of Israel, full of grace and mercy and truth.

It is He that cometh to take away the sins of the world.

Yea, the sins of every man who steadfastly believe on His name.

—Robert D. Hales

Brothers and sisters, one of the great consolations of this Easter season is that because Jesus walked such a long, lonely path utterly alone, we do not have to do so. His solitary journey brought great company for our little version of that path—the merciful care of our Father in Heaven, the unfailing companionship of this Beloved Son, the consummate gift of the Holy Ghost, angels in heaven, family members on both sides of the veil, prophets and apostles, teachers, leaders, friends. All of these and more have been given as companions for our mortal journey because of the Atonement of Jesus Christ and the Restoration of His gospel. Trumpeted from the summit of Calvary is the truth that we will never be left alone nor unaided, even if sometimes we may feel that we are. Truly the Redeemer of us all said: "I will not leave you comfortless: [My Father and] I will come to you [and abide with you]."

—Jeffrey R. Holland

The reason why only Christ can so affect us and how he does it are best made clear in the Book of Mormon. Very early in his translation of that ancient record, Joseph Smith uses a word that takes us right to the heart of the matter. Nephi, seeking confirmation of his father's spiritual experiences, is given a remarkable vision of the coming of Christ, still six hundred years in the future, in which Christ and his mission are referred to as "the condescension of God!… the Redeemer of the world" (1 Nephi 11:16, 26–27). The word chosen there is crucial: *condescension* has come to mean, in our time, treating a supposed inferior in false generosity. It corresponds to the word *patronizing*. But this is clearly not what the angel speaking to Nephi meant. Instead, that unusual term *condescension* was chosen to convey precisely the original meaning given by its Latin roots, *con plus descendere,* that is, "to descend with": Christ, as representing "the condescension of God," is the descending of God with us into all that we experience, including our sin and estrangement, and this is the heart of Christ's mission, the source of his unique power to achieve At One Ment.

—Eugene England

By utilizing the Atonement, we access the gifts of the Holy Ghost, which "filleth with hope and perfect love." None of us can afford to be without that needed hope and love in the treks through our Sinais of circumstance!

—Neal A. Maxwell

I suspect that many Church members are much more familiar with the nature of the redeeming and cleansing power of the Atonement than they are with the strengthening and enabling power. It is one thing to know that Jesus Christ came to earth to die for us~ that is fundamental and foundational to

the doctrine of Christ.
But we also need
to appreciate that the
Lord desires, through
His Atonement and
by the power of the
Holy Ghost, to live
in us~not only to
direct us but also to
empower us.

—David A. Bednar

We see ourselves in terms of yesterday and today, our Heavenly Father sees us in terms of forever. Although we might settle for less, Heavenly Father won't, for He sees us as the glorious beings we are capable of becoming. The gospel of Jesus Christ is a gospel of transformation which takes us men and women of the earth and refines us into men and women for eternities.

—Joseph B. Wirthlin

One of God's greatest gifts to us is the joy of trying again,
for no failure ever need be final.

—Thomas S. Monson

Just as chalk can be removed from a blackboard, with sincere repentance, the effects of our transgression can be erased through the atonement of Jesus Christ.

—Boyd K. Packer

Rev'rently and meekly now,
Let thy head most humbly bow.
Think of me, thou ransomed one;
Think what I for thee have done.
With my blood that dripped like rain,
Sweat in agony of pain,
With my body on the tree
I have ransomed even thee.

At the throne I intercede;
For thee ever do I plead.
I have loved thee as thy friend,
With a love that cannot end.
Be obedient, I implore,
Prayerful, watchful evermore,
And be constant unto me,
That thy Savior I may be.

—"Reverently and Meekly Now"

He is despised and rejected of men; a man of sorrows, and acquainted with grief: and we hid as it were our faces from him; he was despised, and we esteemed him not. Surely he hath borne our griefs, and carried our sorrows: yet we did esteem him stricken, smitten of God, and afflicted. But he was wounded for our transgressions, he was bruised for our iniquities: the chastisement of our peace was upon him; and with his stripes we are healed. All we like sheep have gone astray; we have turned every one to his own way; and the Lord hath laid on

him the iniquity of us all. He was oppressed, and he was afflicted, yet he opened not his mouth: he is brought as a lamb to the slaughter, and as a sheep before her shearers is dumb, so he openeth not his mouth. He was taken from prison and from judgment: and who shall declare his generation? for he was cut off out of the land of the living: for the transgression of my people was he stricken.

—Isaiah 53:3–8

I witness the reality and divinity of a living savior who invites us to come unto Him and be transformed. We can be spiritually prepared and cleansed from sin. Immersed in and saturated with His gospel and purified and sealed by the Holy Spirit of Promise. Even born again.

—David A. Bednar

The cornerstone of God's plan is the Atonement of the Lord Jesus Christ. . . . Remember that the Son of the Highest descended below all and took upon Him our offenses, sins, transgressions, sicknesses, pains, afflictions, and loneliness.

—Hugo Montoya

Uniquely, atoning Jesus also “descended below all things, in that he comprehended all things.” How deep that descent into despair and abysmal agony must have been! He did it to rescue us and in order to comprehend human suffering. Therefore, let us not resent those tutoring experiences which can develop our own empathy further.

—Neal A. Maxwell

I am not a saint, unless you think of a saint as a sinner who keeps on trying.

—Nelson Mandela

Our Savior . . . knows our struggles, our heartaches, our temptations, and our suffering, for He willingly experienced them all as an essential part of His Atonement. And because of this, His Atonement empowers Him to succor us~to give us the strength to bear it all.

—Dallin H. Oaks

Our understanding of and faith in the Atonement of Jesus Christ will provide strength and capacity needed for a successful life. It will also bring confidence in times of trial and peace in moments of turmoil.

—Richard G. Scott

However late you think you are, however many chances you think you have missed, however many mistakes you feel you have made or talents you think you don't have, or however far from home and family and God you feel you have traveled, I testify that you have not traveled beyond the reach of divine love. It is not possible for you to sink lower than the infinite light of Christ's Atonement shines.

—Jeffrey R. Holland

And behold, this is the whole meaning of the law, every whit pointing to that great and last sacrifice; and that great and last sacrifice will be the Son of God, yea, infinite and eternal. And thus he shall bring salvation to all those who shall believe on his name; this being the intent of this last sacrifice, to bring about the bowels of mercy, which overpowereth justice, and bringeth about means unto men that they may have faith unto repentance. And thus mercy can satisfy the demands of justice, and encircles them in the arms of safety, while he that exercises no faith unto repentance is exposed to the whole law of the demands of justice; therefore only unto him that has faith unto repentance is brought about the great and eternal plan of redemption.

—Alma 34:13–16

The prophet Nephi made an important contribution to our understanding of God's grace when he declared, "We labor diligently … to persuade our children, and also our brethren, to believe in Christ, and to be reconciled to God; for we know that it is by grace that we are saved, after all we can do."

However, I wonder if sometimes we misinterpret the phrase "after all we can do."

We must understand that "after" does not equal "because."

We are not saved "because" of all that we can do. Have any of us done all that we can do? Does God wait until we've expended every effort before He will intervene in our lives with His saving grace?

Many people feel discouraged because they constantly fall short. They know firsthand that "the spirit indeed is willing, but the flesh is weak." They raise their voices with Nephi in proclaiming, "My soul grieveth because of mine iniquities."

I am certain Nephi knew that the Savior's grace allows and enables us to overcome sin. This is why Nephi labored so diligently to persuade his children and brethren "to believe in Christ, and to be reconciled to God." After all, that is what we can do! And that is our task in mortality!

—Dieter F. Uchtdorf

No mortal mind can adequately conceive, nor can human tongue appropriately express, the full significance of all that Jesus Christ has done for our Heavenly Father's children through His Atonement. Yet it is vital that we each learn what we can about it. . . . Your understanding of

the Atonement and the insight it provides for your life will greatly enhance your productive use of all of the knowledge, experience, and skills you acquire in mortal life.

—Richard G. Scott

Who shall separate us from the love of Christ? shall tribulation, or distress, or persecution, or famine, or nakedness, or peril, or sword? For I am persuaded, that neither death, nor life, nor angels, nor principalities, nor powers, nor things present, nor things to come, Nor height, nor depth, nor any other creature, shall be able to separate us from the love of God, which is in Christ Jesus our Lord.

—Romans 8:35; 38–39

In His mercy, God promises forgiveness when we repent and turn from wickedness—so much so that our sins will not even be mentioned to us. For us, because of the Atonement of Christ and our repentance, we can look at our past deeds and say, "'Twas I; but 'tis not I." No matter how wicked, we can say, "That's who I was. But that past wicked self is no longer who I am."

—Dale G. Renlund

At this very moment, someone is saying, "Brother Andersen, you don't understand. You can't feel what I have felt. It is too difficult to change." You are correct; I don't fully understand. But there is One who does. He knows. He has felt your pain. He has declared, "I have graven thee upon the palms of my hands." The Savior is there, reaching out to each of us, bidding us: "Come unto me."

—Neil L. Andersen

Wherefore, redemption cometh in and through the Holy Messiah; for he is full of grace and truth. Behold, he offereth himself a sacrifice for sin, to answer the ends of the law, unto all those who have a broken heart and a contrite spirit; and unto none else can the ends of the law be answered. Wherefore, how great the importance to make these things known unto the inhabitants of the earth, that they may know that there is no flesh that can dwell in the presence of God, save it be through the merits, and mercy, and grace of the Holy Messiah, who layeth down his life according to the flesh, and taketh it again by the power of the Spirit, that he may bring to pass the resurrection of the dead, being the first that should rise. Wherefore, he is the firstfruits unto God, inasmuch as he shall make intercession for all the children of men; and they that believe in him shall be saved.

—2 Nephi 2:6–9

He died not for men, but for each man. If each man had been the only man made, He would have done no less.

—C.S. Lewis

Several scriptures describe the essence of that glorious and rescuing Atonement, including a breathtaking, autobiographical verse confiding how Jesus "would that I might not drink the bitter cup, and shrink." Since the "infinite atonement"

required infinite suffering, the risk of recoil was there! All humanity hung on the hinge of Christ's character! Mercifully, He did not shrink but "finished [His] preparations unto the children of men."

—Neal A. Maxwell

The Atonement, which can reclaim each one of us, bears no scars. That means that no matter what we have done or where we have been or how something happened, if we truly repent, He has promised that He would atone. And when He atoned, that settled that. There are so many of us who are thrashing around . . . with feelings of guilt, not knowing quite how to escape. You escape by accepting the Atonement of Christ, and all that was heartache can turn to beauty and love and eternity.

—Linda S. Reeves

In mortality we have the certainty of death and the burden of sin. The Atonement of Jesus Christ offsets these two certainties of mortal life. But apart from death and sin, we have many other challenges as we struggle through mortality. Because of that same Atonement, our Savior can provide us the strength we need to overcome these mortal challenges.

—Dallin H. Oaks

[The Savior] had no debt to pay. He had committed no wrong. Nevertheless, an accumulation of all of the guilt, the grief and sorrow, the pain and humiliation, all of the mental, emotional, and physical torments known to man—He experienced them all.

—Boyd K. Packer

As for the wickedness of the wicked, he shall not fall thereby in the day that he turneth from his wickedness. . . .

… If he turn from his sin, and do that which is lawful and right;

… Restore the pledge, give again that he had robbed, walk in the statutes of life, without committing iniquity; he shall surely live. . . .

None of his sins that he hath committed shall be mentioned unto him: he hath done that which is lawful and right.

—Ezekiel 33:12, 14–16

In striving for some peace and understanding in these difficult matters, it is crucial to remember that we are living—and chose to live—in a fallen world where for divine purposes our pursuit of godliness will be tested and tried again and again. Of greatest assurance in God's plan is that a Savior was promised, a Redeemer, who through our faith in Him would lift us triumphantly over those tests and trials, even though the cost to do so would be unfathomable for both the Father who sent Him and the Son who came. It is only an appreciation of this divine love that will make our own lesser suffering first bearable, then understandable, and finally redemptive.

—Jeffrey R. Holland

We invite everyone on this beautiful planet to taste of His doctrine and see if it is not sweet and good and precious. We ask those of sincere heart to learn of this doctrine and ask their Father in Heaven if it is not true. By doing so, all can discover, embrace, and walk in the true faith of their Father which faith will make them whole.

—Dieter F. Uchtdorf

The pleasing word of God invites us to use the power of the Atonement of Christ to apply it to ourselves and become reconciled with His will—and not with the will of the devil and the flesh—so we, through His grace, can be saved.

—Francisco J. Viñas

Mortal experience points evermore to the Atonement of Jesus Christ as the central act of all human history. The more I learn and experience, the more unselfish, stunning, and encompassing His Atonement becomes!

—Neal A. Maxwell

Father said he needed
someone who had enough love
To give his life so we all could
return there above.
There was another who sought for
the honor divine.
Jesus said, "Father, send me, and
the glory be thine."

—"I Lived in Heaven"

It is not a sign of weakness to abandon pseudo-self-reliance and avail ourselves of the Atonement; rather it is a gesture of deep gratitude, love, and humility, faith and courage. The Atonement not only allows for repentance of sin but also permits us to forgive ourselves and receive the outpouring of his grace that strengthens and helps us when we simply do not have the power to overcome our human weaknesses on our own. A greater understanding of and faith in the power of the Atonement brings our lives into spiritual balance by allowing the Savior to share our burdens and compensate for our many inadequacies (see Matthew 11:28; Ether 12:27).

—Brent and Wendy Top

185

And he shall go forth, suffering pains and afflictions and temptations of every kind; and this that the word might be fulfilled which saith he will take upon him the pains and the sicknesses of his people. And he will take upon him death, that he may loose the bands of death which bind his people; and he will take upon him their infirmities, that his bowels may be filled with mercy, according to the flesh, that he may know according to the flesh how to succor his people according to their infirmities. Now the Spirit knoweth all things; nevertheless the Son of God suffereth according to the flesh that he might take upon him the sins of his people, that he might blot out their transgressions according to the power of his deliverance; and now behold, this is the testimony which is in me.

—Alma 7:11–13

Jesus, once of humble birth,
Now in glory comes to earth.
Once he suffered grief and pain;
Now he comes on earth to reign.
Once a meek and lowly Lamb,
Now the Lord, the great I Am.
Once upon the cross he bowed;
Now his chariot is the cloud.
Once he groaned in blood and tears;
Now in glory he appears.
Once rejected by his own,
Now their King he shall be known.
Once forsaken, left alone,
Now exalted to a throne.
Once all things he meekly bore,
But he now will bear no more.
But he now will bear no more.

—"Jesus, Once of Humble Birth"

I ask you, what father and mother could stand by and listen to the cry of their children in distress, in this world, and not render aid and assistance? I have heard of mothers throwing themselves into raging streams when they could not swim a stroke to save their drowning children, rushing into burning buildings to rescue those whom they loved. . . . [Our Father] saw [His] Son finally upon Calvary; he saw his body stretched out upon the wooden cross; he saw the cruel nails driven through hands and feet, and the blows that broke the skin, tore the flesh, and let out the life's blood of his Son. He looked upon that. . . . His Father looked on with great grief and agony over his Beloved Son, until there seems to have come a moment when even our Savior cried out in despair: "My God, my God, why hast thou forsaken me?"

In that hour I think I can see our dear Father behind the veil looking upon these dying struggles until even he could not endure it any longer; and, like the mother who bids farewell to her dying child, has to be taken out of the room, so as not to look upon the last struggles, so he bowed his head, and hid in some part of his universe, his great heart almost breaking for the love that he had for his Son. Oh, in that moment when he might have saved his Son, I thank him and praise him that he did not fail us, for he had not only the love of his Son in mind, but he also had love for us. I rejoice that he did not interfere, and that his love for us made it possible for him to endure to look upon the sufferings of his Son and give him finally to us, our Savior and our Redeemer. Without him, without his sacrifice, we would have remained, and we would never have come glorified into his presence. And so this is what it cost, in part, for our Father in Heaven to give the gift of his Son unto men.

—Jeffrey R. Holland

For the atonement
satisfieth the demands
of his justice upon all
those who have not the
law given to them, that
they are delivered from
that awful monster,
death and hell, and the
devil, and the lake of fire
and brimstone, which is
endless torment;

and they are restored to that God who gave them breath, which is the Holy One of Israel.

—2 Nephi 9:26

Moroni confirmed: "What is it that ye shall hope for? Behold I say unto you that ye shall have hope through the atonement of Christ." Real hope, therefore, is not associated with things mercurial, but rather with things immortal and eternal!

—Neal A. Maxwell

Through the power of the atonement of Jesus Christ our natures can be changed then our power to carry burdens can be increased more than enough.

—HENRY B. EYRING

Most of us clearly understand that the Atonement is for sinners. I am not so sure, however, that we know and understand that the Atonement is also for saints—for good men and women who are obedient, worthy, and conscientious and who are striving to become better.

—DAVID A. BEDNAR

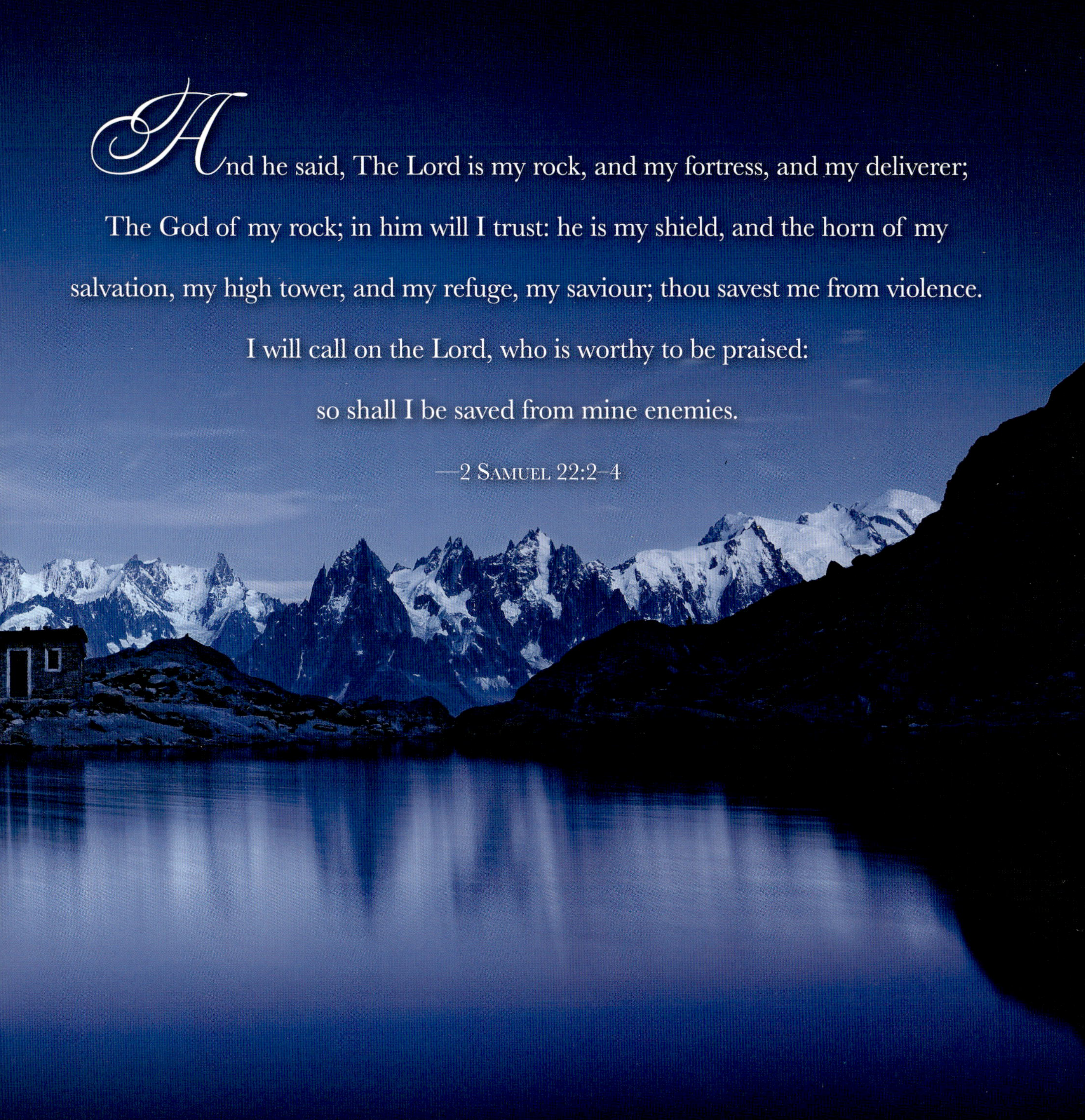
And he said, The Lord is my rock, and my fortress, and my deliverer;
The God of my rock; in him will I trust: he is my shield, and the horn of my
salvation, my high tower, and my refuge, my saviour; thou savest me from violence.
I will call on the Lord, who is worthy to be praised:
so shall I be saved from mine enemies.
—2 Samuel 22:2–4

Our Savior's Atonement does more than assure us of immortality by a universal resurrection and give us the opportunity to be cleansed from sin by repentance and baptism. His Atonement also provides the opportunity to call upon Him who has experienced all of our mortal infirmities to give us the strength to bear the burdens of mortality. He knows of our anguish, and He is there for us. . . . The healing and strengthening power of Jesus Christ and His Atonement is for all of us who will ask.

—Dallin H. Oaks

For all have sinned, and come short of the glory of God; Being justified freely by his grace through the redemption that is in Christ Jesus:

—Romans 3:23–24

As we progress along the covenant path, we will make mistakes. . . . We fail only if we fail to take another faithful step forward. We will not, we cannot, fail if we are faithfully yoked to the Savior—He who has never failed and will never fail us!

—Randall K. Bennett

Trust in the merits and in the power of the Atonement of Jesus Christ. Through His atoning sacrifice, we can gain the courage to win all the wars of our time, even in the midst of our difficulties, challenges, and temptations. Let us trust in His love and power to save us.

—Ulisses Soares

The Savior's Atonement cannot become commonplace in our teaching, in our conversation, or in our hearts. It is sacred and holy, for it was through this "great and last sacrifice" that Jesus the Christ brought "salvation to all those who shall believe on his name" (Alma 34:10, 15).

—Dieter F. Uchtdorf

It was the witness of the Spirit of the coming Atonement which saw Job through the tests life is intended to include for all of us. That is part of the great plan of happiness the Father gave us. He allowed His Son to provide, by His atoning sacrifice, the hope that comforts us no matter how hard the way home to Him may be.

—Henry B. Eyring

That first Easter sequence of Atonement and Resurrection constitutes the most consequential moment, the most generous gift, the most excruciating pain, and the most majestic manifestation of pure love ever to be demonstrated in the history of this world. Jesus Christ, the Only Begotten Son of God, suffered, died, and rose from death in order that He could, like lightning in a summer storm, grasp us as we fall, hold us with His might, and through our obedience to His commandments, lift us to eternal life.

—Jeffrey R. Holland

Ultimate hope . . .
is tied to Jesus and the
blessings of the great
Atonement, blessings
resulting in the universal
Resurrection and the
precious opportunity
provided thereby for us
to practice emancipating
repentance, making
possible what the
scriptures call "a perfect
brightness of hope."

—Neal A. Maxwell